CONTENTS

T0004840

WHAT ARE DRONES?

Drones are all over the news these days, but what is a drone? Put simply, a drone is an unmanned **vehicle**. Today, drones have become a fun hobby. You can go to your local toy or hobby store and buy a drone that you can fly yourself.

Historically, the military used drones for **surveillance** and combat, or active fighting. Because drones don't have a person onboard to direct them, they are perfect for missions, or tasks, that could be too unsafe, time-consuming, or unpleasant for humans.

DRONES ARE EVERYWHERE!

DRONES IN SPACE

DANIEL R. FAUST

PowerKiDS
press.

Published in 2020 by The Rosen Publishing Group, Inc.
29 East 21st Street, New York, NY 10010

Copyright © 2020 by The Rosen Publishing Group, Inc.

All rights reserved. No part of this book may be reproduced in any form without permission in writing from the publisher, except by a reviewer.

First Edition

Editor: Shannon Harts
Book Design: Tanya Dellaccio

Photo Credits: Cover (drone) https://upload.wikimedia.org/wikipedia/commons/a/aa/Aff-tech-demonstrator-prototype_1.jpg; cover (background) Witthaya Prasongsin/Moment/Getty Images; series background Djem/Shuttertock.com; p. 5 Dominic Hart/Don Richey/NASA Image Library; p. 7 (main) Ethan Miller/Getty Images News/Getty Images; p. 7 (inset) John Moore/Getty Images News/Getty Images; p. 9 NASA/JPL-Caltech/NASA Image Library; p. 11 TASS/Getty Images; p. 13 (main) NASA/JPLCaltech/SwRI/MSSS/Gerald Eichstadt/Sean Doran/NASA Image Library; p. 13 (inset) NASA/NASA Image Library; p. 15 NASA/Getty Images News/Getty Images; p. 17 (main) NASA/JPL-Caltech/University of Arizona/Texas A&M University/NASA Image Library; p. 17 (inset) NASA/JPL-Caltech/NASA Image Library; p. 19 Patrick T. Fallon/Bloomberg/Getty Images; p. 21 (main) NASA/Getty Images; p. 21 NASA/NASA Image Library.

Cataloging-in-Publication Data

Names: Faust, Daniel R.
Title: Drones in space / Daniel R. Faust.
Description: New York : PowerKids Press, 2020. | Series: Drones are everywhere! | Includes glossary and index.
Identifiers: ISBN 9781725309388 (pbk.) | ISBN 9781725309401 (library bound) | ISBN 9781725309395 (6 pack)
Subjects: LCSH: Drone aircraft-Juvenile literature.
Classification: LCC UG1242.D7 F38 2020 | DDC 623.74'69-dc23

Manufactured in the United States of America

CPSIA Compliance Information: Batch #CWPK20. For Further Information contact Rosen Publishing, New York, New York at 1-800-237-9932.

Flying quadcopters, named for the four rotors that move them through the air, has become a popular pastime for children and adults.

Whether they're large or small, or used for fun or to help keep people safe, many drones work the same. Drones are usually built from plastics or lightweight metals, such as aluminum. They often have cameras and sensors that let a person controlling them from the ground see what the drone "sees."

Some drones have onboard computers and can be programmed, or set, to move in certain directions. Most drones are powered using **batteries**, but some use solar panels, or instruments that turn the sun's light into electricity.

DRONE DETAILS

WHILE SOME DRONES ARE CONTROLLED USING LARGE CONSOLES, OR COMPUTERS THAT CONTAIN CONTROLS FOR FARAWAY MACHINES, OTHER DRONES ARE DIRECTED USING REMOTE CONTROLS, OR HANDHELD INSTRUMENTS THAT LOOK LIKE VIDEO GAME CONTROLLERS.

Some military drones, like the MQ-1B Predator, are armed with missiles, or objects that can be thrown, shot, or sent out to fight an enemy.

DRONE DIFFICULTIES

The heavy spacesuits that astronauts, or people who travel into space, wear guard them from many dangers. Unlike humans, drones don't need to worry as much about unsafe conditions, **solar radiation**, or the lack of air.

One of the biggest difficulties, or challenges, drones face in space is **propulsion**. The rotors of a quadcopter drone will not work in space or on other planets. Drones will need to have a new way to move. **Engineers** are making drones that will use jets of oxygen or water **vapor** to carefully move through space.

DRONE DETAILS

SPACE IS COLD! WITHOUT THE WARMTH OF EARTH'S ATMOSPHERE—THE MASS OF AIR SURROUNDING EARTH—OR A SPACESUIT, ASTRONAUTS FACE TEMPERATURES THAT ARE SEVERAL HUNDRED DEGREES BELOW FREEZING.

NASA announced in 2018 that a special drone would be sent to Mars on a mission, or spacecraft flight to perform a certain task, planned for 2020.

BY AIR OR BY LAND

A large majority of drones are unmanned aerial vehicles, or UAVs—aerial meaning they're used in the air. The familiar quadcopter that's popular with **civilian** drone flyers and the airplane-like drones the military uses are UAVs. But not all drones fly. Unmanned ground vehicles, or UGVs, are a lot like their flying cousins.

UGVs are designed, or made, to be controlled from a distance to perform dangerous tasks, like **reconnaissance** in enemy territory or getting rid of bombs. Like aerial drones, some UGVs are armed for active fighting settings.

While not as well-known as aerial drones, UGVs like the Scarabey are saving soldiers' lives on the battlefield. These drones are used for surveillance, active fighting, and to find explosives.

PROBES AND ROVERS

Like the drones we use on Earth, drones made for space can be either UAVs or UGVs. The unmanned aerial vehicles that NASA sends to explore, or study, moons, asteroids, and other planets are more commonly called probes.

Probes fly over the surface of the area to be studied, taking pictures and videos, and gathering information about things like radiation and the atmosphere. Probes can tell us a lot about other places in our solar system, but sometimes astronauts need to get up close and personal.

Probes, like the Juno spacecraft that was sent to explore Jupiter, usually only orbit, or circle, the body they are studying. Some probes may enter the planet's atmosphere, but they are not prepared to work on the planet's surface.

There are two kinds of planets in our solar system. The inner planets, like Earth and Mars, are solid and rocky. They are known as **terrestrial** planets. The outer planets, like Jupiter and Saturn, are mostly made of gases like helium and hydrogen.

While probes are perfect for exploring these gas giants, UGVs called rovers can be used to explore the surface of terrestrial planets. Rovers, like the ones NASA has sent to Mars, can collect rock samples and explore caves that probes can't reach.

DRONE DETAILS

SOJOURNER WAS THE FIRST MARS ROVER, SENT IN 1996. SPIRIT & OPPORTUNITY LANDED IN 2004 AND LOOKED FOR WATER. IN 2011, CURIOSITY WAS SENT TO SEE IF MARS COULD HAVE ONCE SUPPORTED LIFE.

Mars rovers are equipped, or supplied, with everything they need to explore the Red Planet, including cameras, a tool-outfitted arm, and solar panels.

TEAMWORK

NASA may have been thinking of the old saying, "two heads are better than one," when it started planning its next mission to Mars.

NASA's Mars 2020 rover mission is scheduled to include a UAV called the Mars Helicopter in addition to the ground-based rover. The rover will carry the UAV until a suitable launch, or take off, site can be found. Once in the air, the Mars Helicopter will be able to explore places that a rover can't go, like the inside of **volcanoes** and craters.

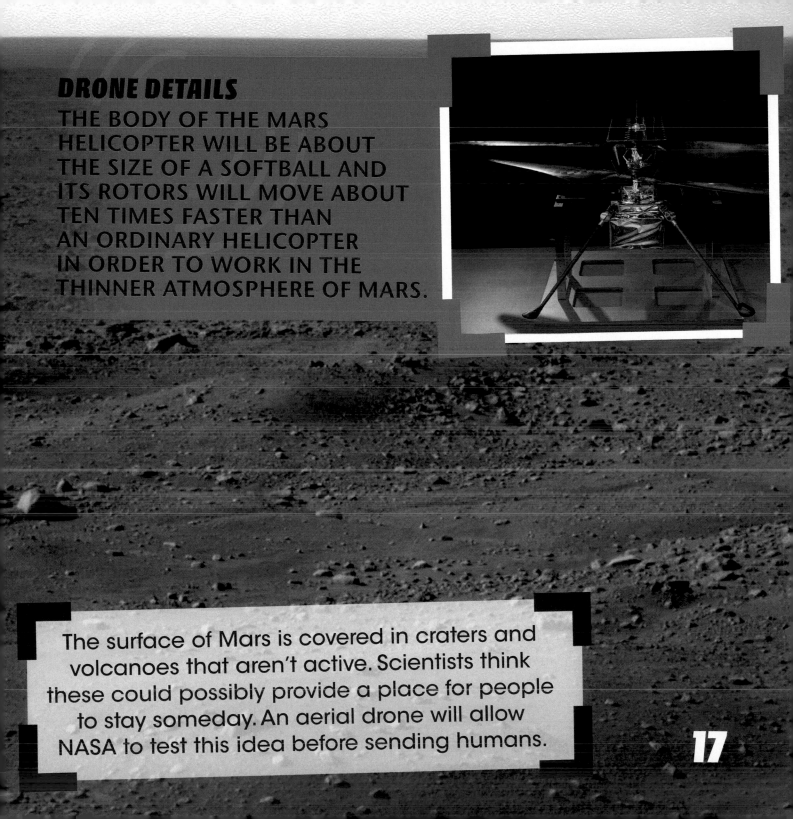

DRONE DETAILS

THE BODY OF THE MARS HELICOPTER WILL BE ABOUT THE SIZE OF A SOFTBALL AND ITS ROTORS WILL MOVE ABOUT TEN TIMES FASTER THAN AN ORDINARY HELICOPTER IN ORDER TO WORK IN THE THINNER ATMOSPHERE OF MARS.

The surface of Mars is covered in craters and volcanoes that aren't active. Scientists think these could possibly provide a place for people to stay someday. An aerial drone will allow NASA to test this idea before sending humans.

CARGO AND CAMERAS

In addition to missions of exploration, space agencies, or government departments like NASA, use drones to haul cargo, or goods, into Earth's orbit. The Dragon is a reusable unmanned spacecraft that SpaceX built and operates. The Dragon is used to carry cargo from Earth to the International Space Station, or ISS.

The ISS is the home of the Int-Ball, a small autonomous, or independently acting, drone. It was created to help astronauts document, or keep track of, their work by following them and taking videos or pictures.

DRONE DETAILS

THE U.S. MILITARY'S X-37B IS AN UNMANNED SPACECRAFT THAT LOOKS LIKE A SMALL SPACE SHUTTLE. THE X-37B WAS LAUNCHED, OR SENT OUT, IN APRIL 2010 AND SPENT SEVERAL MONTHS IN ORBIT BEFORE RETURNING TO EARTH.

Astronauts must document every step of their work to make sure there are no mistakes. But, taking video and pictures takes time. A drone with cameras gives astronauts more time for other important tasks.

ASTEROID MINING

Between Mars and Jupiter, there is a giant ring of asteroids. This asteroid belt has between one and two million asteroids that are larger than 3,200 feet (975 m) in **diameter**. Since asteroids are little more than big rocks, they could provide a supply of iron, gold, and other valuable, or expensive, metals.

Rovers could be sent to these asteroids to extract, or remove, valuable rocks someday. Some asteroids might even have a form of water, which could help explain how asteroid crashes can cause life on planets.

In addition to the asteroid belt between Mars and Jupiter, a region of space beyond Neptune called the Kuiper Belt also contains a large number of asteroids that could one day be mined for important metals.

BEYOND MARS

With rovers exploring the surface of Mars and drones someday acting as robotic **prospectors** in the asteroid belt, what could possibly come next for unmanned aerial and ground vehicles in space?

Well, NASA is already in the early stages of making a spacecraft, called Dragonfly, that will explore the surface of Titan, one of Saturn's moons. Although any probe launched from Earth would take around 10 years to reach Titan, it's exciting to think that drones will allow us to continue exploring faraway planets and moons.

GLOSSARY

battery: An instrument placed inside a machine to supply it with electricity.

civilian: A person who is not a part of the military or a police force.

diameter: The distance through the center of something from one side to the other.

engineer: Someone who plans and builds machines.

propulsion: The force that moves something forward.

prospectors: People who search an area for gold, minerals, and other valuable resources.

reconnaissance: The act of obtaining information about an enemy or a potential enemy.

solar radiation: The radiation, or energy, the sun gives off.

surveillance: Continuous observation of a person, place, or group in order to gather information.

terrestrial: Earth-like in form or appearance.

vapor: Something that is in the form of a gas.

vehicle: A machine used to carry goods from one place to another.

volcano: An opening in a planet's surface through which hot, liquid rock sometimes flows.

INDEX

WEBSITES

Due to the changing nature of Internet links, PowerKids Press has developed an online list of websites related to the subject of this book. This site is updated regularly. Please use this link to access the list: www.powerkidslinks.com/dae/space